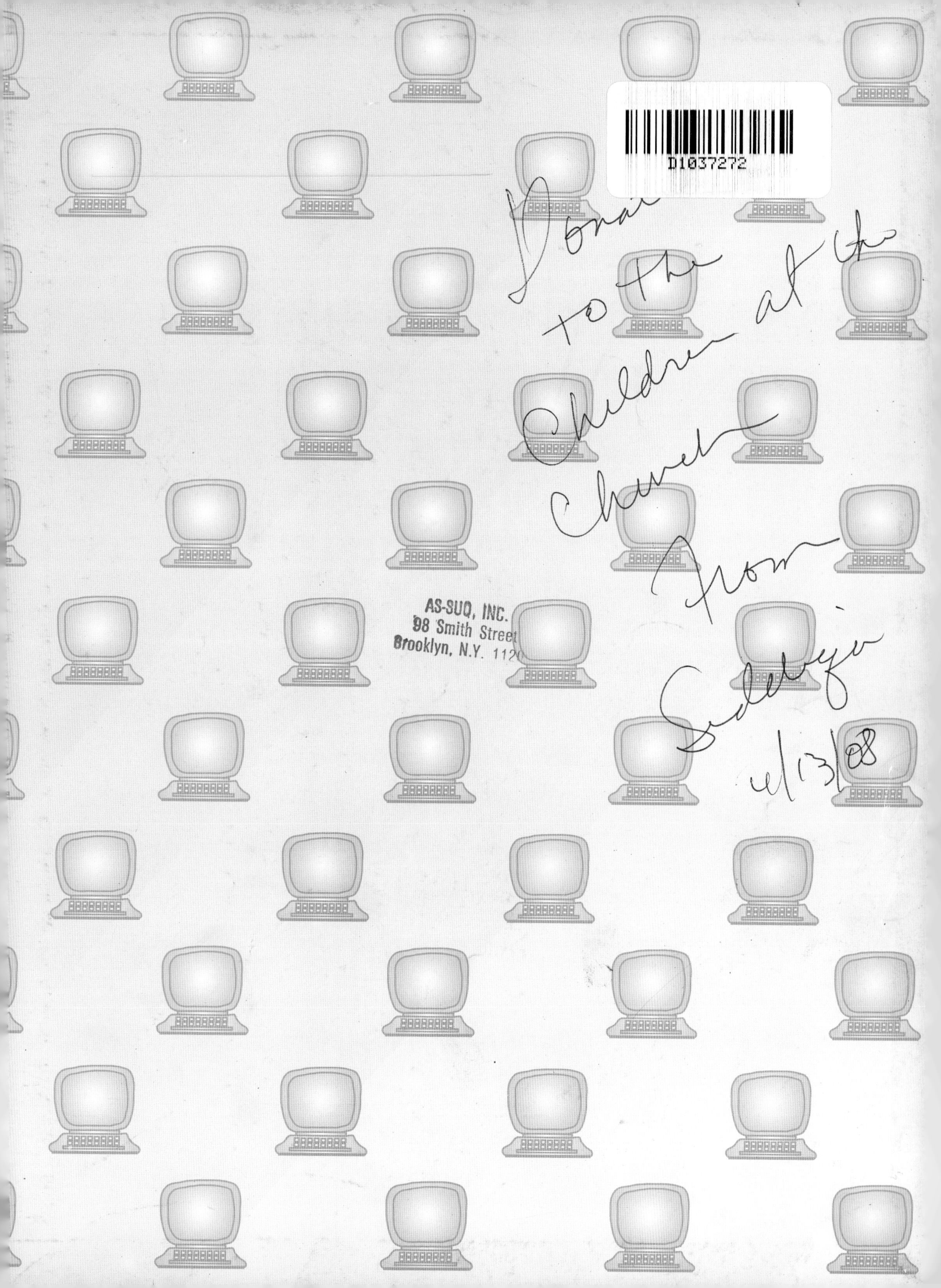
D1037272

Written by:

Awad Mansour, Ph. D.
Ali Rumman

Translated from Arabic by:

Mohammed Mahmoued Dabbour

Illustrated by:

Rashid Al-Kabariti

Edited by:

Lynda Young
Mohammad M. "Minhaj" Khokhar

Book Design:

Amica Design

Library of Congress Catalog Number: 94-71602

A JOURNEY TO THE WORLD OF COMPUTERS
A COMPUTER READER FOR KIDS
A JOINT PROJECT OF NAMA INC. AND AMICA INTERNATIONAL

Published in Seattle, WA

ISBN # 1-884187-06-4

Published and Distributed by:
AMICA INTERNATIONAL
1201 First Avenue S.
Suite 203
Seattle, WA 98134
Tel: (206) 467-1035 • Fax: (206) 467-1522
Outside Seattle: 1 (800) 622-9256

A COMPUTER READER FOR KIDS

AMICA PUBLISHING HOUSE
Seattle

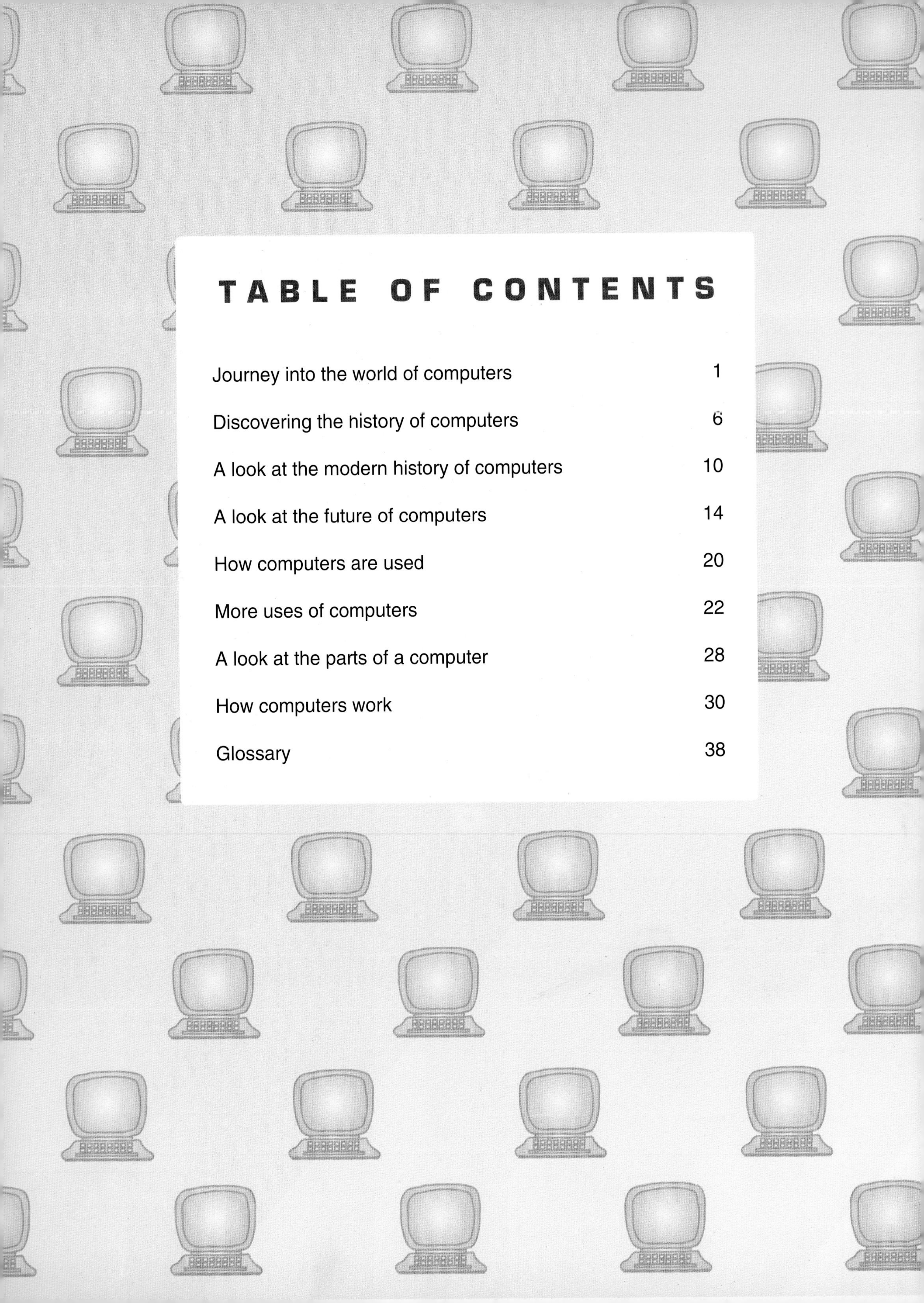

TABLE OF CONTENTS

Journey into the world of computers

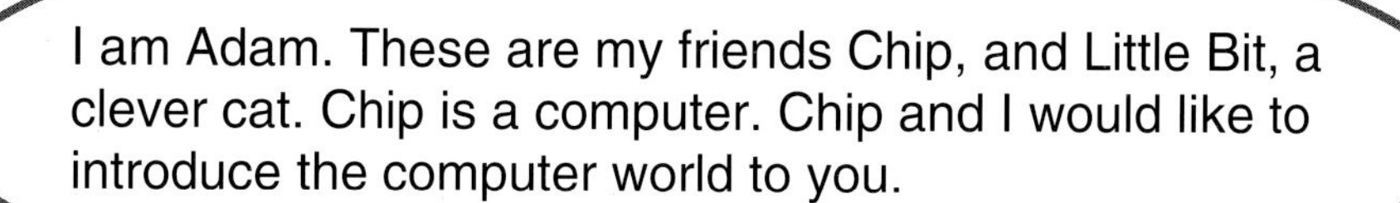

COMPUTERS help you talk on the telephone.
Computers give you ARCADE GAMES to play.
Computers control the flight of airplanes.
The words of this book were typed into a computer.
Computers help your doctor.
Computers create special effects for your favorite movies.
Chip, what is a computer? Can you show me?
Put in the FLOPPY DISK and look at my DISPLAY. To ACCESS the information, touch any key on my KEYBOARD and let's begin.

Okay! Come on Adam, press the keys.
QUESTIONS:
1. Is a computer smarter than people?
2. Does a computer think like people do?
3. Do you have to have a lot of knowledge in mathematics and science to use a computer?
ANSWERS:
1. No. 2. No. 3. No.
What else can you tell me about computers?
A computer is fast.
A computer is accurate.
It memorizes a lot of information (called DATA), and it doesn't forget anything.
A computer is a machine that helps people. It does not have emotions or an imagination. It cannot enjoy life as humans can.

Little Bit, here is some of what I have learned.
A computer follows our instructions.
We INPUT information into the computer.
Computers solve problems and answer questions.
Computers can help us draw pictures called GRAPHICS.
A computer cannot do everything by itself. Even the most powerful computer in the world can only follow instructions.
That's just fine, but can a computer make my lunch?

Watch out Chip!
Little Bit will attack!
Let's go to the museum. Uncle Ray works there and we can learn more about computers.
Stop laughing. It looked like lunch to me.

Discovering the history of computers

The sign read:
Press the number 1000, then wait for instructions.
1000

Don't be afraid. It's just a computerized dinosaur.

1000
Press the number 2000 to learn about the events leading up to the invention of the computer.

Man invented a simple counting device called an ABACUS. It helped people add and subtract large numbers.

Continue to follow the
signs to learn more
about the history of
computers.
People have always
searched for knowledge,
and have used
knowledge to invent
things to make life easier.

A look at the modern history of computers

Man's search for knowledge continued. A French man named Blaise PASCAL invented the adding machine in 1641.

The CALCULATOR was invented by a German man named Gottfried LEIBNITZ a few years later. His calculator could add, subtract, multiply, divide, and find square roots of numbers.

The JACQUARD LOOM was invented in 1801 by a French man named Joseph-Marie JACQUARD. He was a weaver, and he wanted to make it easier to weave cloth. He invented an automatic loom. He punched holes in cards and hooked them together to make a pattern. The cards instructed the loom to make the cloth. Jacquard's loom was the first machine to use information to create something.

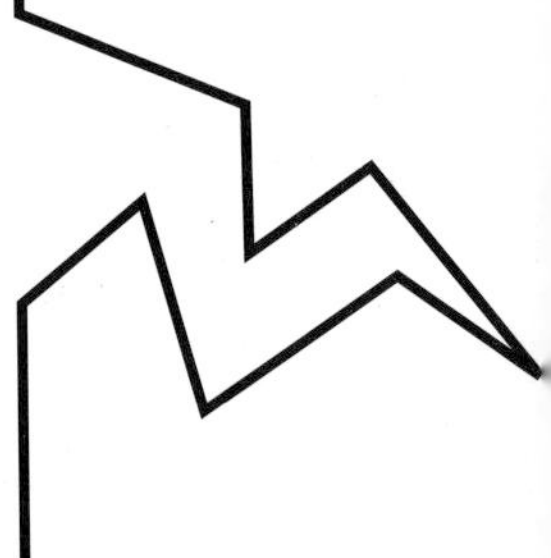

Scientists searched for knowledge, and the world witnessed the INDUSTRIAL REVOLUTION. People invented many machines, and they needed mathematics more than ever before.

Let's go. I'm afraid that I'll fall asleep.

Mark I
This computer was called MARK I. It was invented in 1943 at Harvard University. It used thousands of moving parts and was as big as a room.
Only trained computer scientists could work with computers. The Mark I was several computer generations ago.
What are computer generations?

1st Generation Computers:
Bulky VACUUM TUBES were used. These computers could carry out 1,000 operations per second.
2nd Generation Computers:
TRANSISTORS, which are also used in radios, were invented in 1948. A transistor controls the amount of electric power that flows in and out of a wire. These computers could carry out 10,000 operations a second.
3rd Generation Computers:
The integrated circuit was invented in 1958. Integrated means combined. Integrated circuits held in a small place all the information a computer needs to run. These computers could carry out 1,000,000 operations a second.
4th Generation Computers:
The computer CHIP was invented in 1968. A single computer chip contains thousands of CIRCUITS. These computers carry out ten million operations a second.
Thirty years ago computers were very big, they cost a lot of money, and were difficult to use. Today, many people own a computer. They are much smaller and do not cost as much. Some computers are PORTABLE. You can find computers anywhere you travel.

A look at the future of computers

For example, you will be able to do all of your shopping with a computer. You will not have to leave your house to buy food from the market. You can order the items you want with a computer and the store will have the food delivered to your home. You will also pay for your food through the computer.

A "Super Highway" for computers is being built. It will make it possible for people from all over the world to talk with each other.

The TV in your home will be a powerful computer, you will call it a "Teleputer." You will be able to take classes to learn new languages, look at maps of any city in the world, read newspapers and magazines, and play games with someone in China. In other words, you will learn while playing on a computer. You will be educated and entertained at the same time. It is called "Edutainment."

I can't carry all of these books. Just give me that compact disc (CD for short).
You will be able to read any book you want on your computer screen. You'll not only be able to read, but you will be able to see and hear actual images reading to you. This is called Multimedia.
ENCYCLOPEDIA

So I say to you, my friends, that even though we must face the difficulties of today and tomorrow, I still have a dream. It is a dream deeply rooted in the American dream that one day this nation will rise up and live out the true meaning of its creed—we hold these truths to be self-evident, that all men are created equal.

Your doctor will be able to help you through a computer. You can tell him how you feel and he can tell you what you need to do to feel better. A computer will even be able to give you a shot when you need one.

You will be able to design your own computer games. You will have a choice of what ending you want to see when you are watching your favorite television show.

More and more people will be working on computers out of their homes and will not be going into an office to work. While they are working, they will do exercises with the help of computers to help them stay healthy.

Your oven will know how to cook your favorite foods. You will be able to phone your oven from your car on your way home from work and your food will be ready for you when you get home.

Your car will know what direction you're driving. It will tell you how to get where you're going, and how long it will take.

You will talk to computers and they will be able to talk back. They will be able to recognize your voice and respond only to your commands.

When you play computer games you will be able to play in "Virtual Reality," this means you will wear a helmet when you play that will make you see everything around you as if it were real, but it will be COMPUTER GENERATED and not at all real.

Computers will become faster and faster and will come in all shapes and sizes. They will continue to help you in your day-to-day life more and more. No one knows what computers of the future will be able to do. People are always making computers that are smarter than ever before.
Adam, this search for knowledge will continue for many years to come. What would you like computers to do for you? You can think about that as you continue your journey to the world of computers.

How computers are used

There are many ways to use computers.
38.00
This sewing machine has a tiny computer. The computer tells the sewing machine how to sew many different designs.
There is a little computer inside this camera that tells the camera how to take a picture.
With the help of a computer, this musician's keyboard can sound like 29 different kinds of musical instruments.
Let's go. Music hurts my ears.
Telephones, calculators, electronic dictionaries, typewriters, and many other machines depend on computers.

More uses for computers

We transmit the information via SATELLITE.
This is a computer SIMULATOR. We learn how to steer the ship by looking at the picture the computer has created for us.
I see. That way if anything goes wrong nothing bad will happen to the ship.

How can you tell before you set out on your sea journey what the weather will be like?
Follow me and I will show you.
This computer receives information from satellites and weather stations. It takes photos of clouds, measures wind speed, and records temperatures. It can then tell us what the weather will be.
Let's hit the road, Adam.

Adam! Look!

I'm out of here!

The license plate number is HG 987.

We'll see what is in the computer.

According to our computer this car was reported stolen. Please arrest the driver.
I'm on my way!
Come with me to the police station.

My name is John Jason. I live at 234 Maple Drive.
Mr. Jason, according to our computer you're wanted for stealing a car.
How did you know that?
Am I under arrest Adam?
No, of course you're not. Let's go.

A look at the parts of a computer

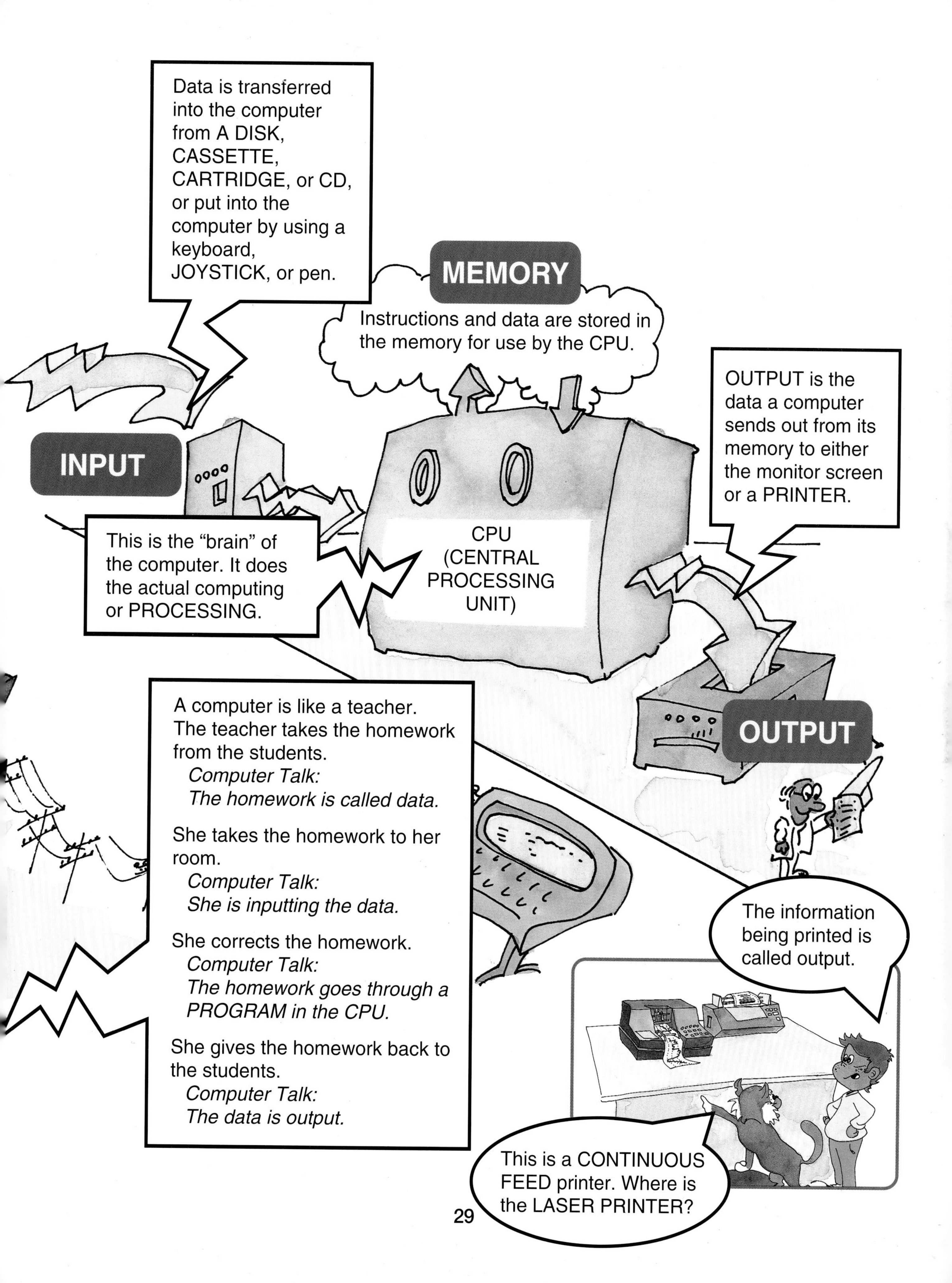
Data is transferred into the computer from A DISK, CASSETTE, CARTRIDGE, or CD, or put into the computer by using a keyboard, JOYSTICK, or pen.
MEMORY
Instructions and data are stored in the memory for use by the CPU.
INPUT
OUTPUT is the data a computer sends out from its memory to either the monitor screen or a PRINTER.
This is the "brain" of the computer. It does the actual computing or PROCESSING.
CPU (CENTRAL PROCESSING UNIT)
OUTPUT
A computer is like a teacher. The teacher takes the homework from the students.
Computer Talk:
The homework is called data.
She takes the homework to her room.
Computer Talk:
She is inputting the data.
She corrects the homework.
Computer Talk:
The homework goes through a PROGRAM in the CPU.
She gives the homework back to the students.
Computer Talk:
The data is output.
The information being printed is called output.
This is a CONTINUOUS FEED printer. Where is the LASER PRINTER?

How computers work

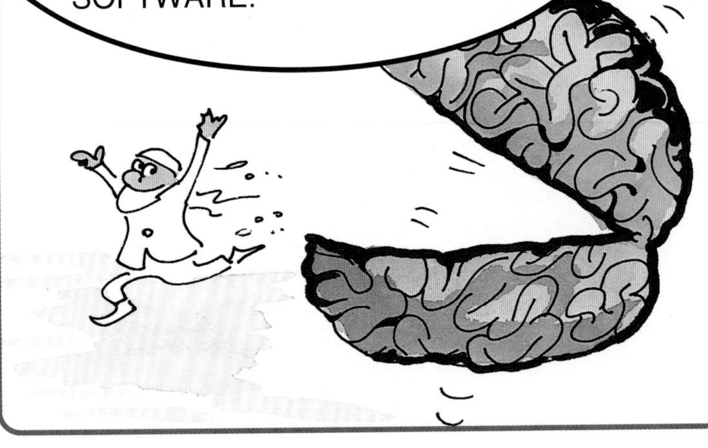

1. Computers have their own language.
2. Computers store information in a memory unit, just like a doctor stores information in his brain.
3. When asked to perform a requested function, the computer looks for the information it needs to perform the function in its memory.

Is a computer better than a human brain?
Our brains are better, but a computer thinks faster and it doesn't forget information.

Does a computer make mistakes?
Wrong information in the program will cause the computer to make mistakes. We say "GIGO" which means Garbage In, Garbage Out.

A robot is not a real person. It is a computer that carries out some human activities. It follows your instructions.
1. Go to the kitchen. 2. Put some tea on the stove.
Here's a program for you. I hope there isn't a BUG in it.

Look how foolish he is! He dropped the tea on the stove!

I think you need to write a better program. Did you SAVE and BACKUP your last program?

Please RUN this program.
1. Fill the kettle with water.
2. Put tea in the kettle.
3. Put the kettle on the stove.

The tea is boiling! Why haven't you taken the kettle off the stove?

Would you like some tea?
No thanks. I don't eat or drink.

You didn't instruct him to take the tea off the stove. A computer will carry out a program step-by-step. If you make even one mistake, or forget something, the program will not work.

Are you a real man?
No. I'm only a computer. I understand computer language.

What is a computer? What is COMPUTER LANGUAGE?
I don't know. I can only carry out orders.

Do you mean that you don't know everything?
Yes. I have to be told what to do.

You can take a break. Adam will LOAD a new program into your memory.

1. Quickly step back.
2. Open the door.
3. Walk out the door.

Oh no! He was carrying out my orders exactly as instructed.
And he CRASHED!

Chip, Little Bit, and I hope you enjoyed your Journey to the World of Computers!
Please visit us again soon!

GLOSSARY

Abacus An ancient Chinese device for adding and subtracting numbers.

Access To get information or DATA from a computer's MEMORY. Accessing information is like looking up something in a dictionary. But it usually takes only a second or two to access information from a computer.

Arcade games A computer that is built to do only one job. It is also called a dedicated computer. Bank teller machines are also dedicated computers.

Backup An extra copy of a file or disk, stored in case something happens to the original.

Bug An error in a computer PROGRAM. A bug in a program has to be fixed so that the program is "bug-free," and will run without errors. Finding and fixing the problem is called "debugging."

Calculator A machine for doing math problems.

Cartridge A plastic case with a ROM chip in it. A cartridge usually fits into an opening in the back or side of a home computer. For example, the ROM chip in a cartridge might contain a game PROGRAM.

Cassette A plastic case with a spool of recording tape in it. A cassette tape, like a CARTRIDGE, might contain a game or some other kind of computer PROGRAM. A cassette used with a computer is similar to a cassette used for music recordings.

Central processing unit The computer's "brain," which carries out commands and controls the other units. Abbreviated CPU.

Character A letter, number, punctuation mark, or symbol.

Chip Chips are tiny parts in a computer that do all the work. There are different chips for different jobs. For example, a chip might contain a computer's MEMORY or control other chips. A single chip contains thousands of electrical pathways or CIRCUITS.

Circuit An electrical pathway. There are many different kinds of circuits in a computer.

Computer A machine that works with, or processes, information or DATA that you give it. The computer uses a PROGRAM that tells it what to do. All the information is stored in the computer's MEMORY.

Computer generated When a computer is used to produce a special effect or product it is computer generated.

Computer language One of the many special languages used for telling the computer what to do. Two types are HIGH-LEVEL LANGUAGE and PROGRAMMING LANGUAGE.

Continuous-feed Computer paper that feeds automatically through a printer as one long sheet.

Crash When the computer suddenly stops working.

Data Information that you INPUT into a computer, or that the computer OUTPUTS.
Small pieces of information that a computer receives, works upon, and sends out.

Disk A round, flat, plastic "record" that is sealed in a square holder. The disk stays in the holder even while it is "played." The disk is used to store a PROGRAM or DATA. They are sometimes called "floppy disks" or "floppies." (See also FLOPPY DISK and HARD DISK.)

Disk drive A computer's disk "player" that runs the disk. It can READ the information on the disk or WRITE new information on the disk. It is a slot for FLOPPY DISKS, or a sealed HARD DISK unit.

Display The information shown by a computer on the MONITOR screen.

Dot-matrix printer A type of PRINTER that uses pins to make ink dots that form letters.

Electronic A type of device that works by shooting electric particles called electrons through a VACUUM TUBE, TRANSISTOR, or INTEGRATED CIRCUIT.

File The place on a DISK where you STORE the DATA you have been working with.

Floppy disk A removable DISK which holds less information than a HARD DISK. It fits into its own DISK DRIVE, and is used to load SOFTWARE and DATA into the computer. Also called a DISKETTE. (See also DISK and HARD DISK.)

GIGO Stands for Garbage In, Garbage Out. It means that if you put wrong information into the computer, wrong information will come out.

Graphics Arranging words and pictures for a pleasing design on a computer screen or on paper.

Hard disk A DISK with a large amount of MEMORY, sealed in its own container and built into the computer. (See also DISK and FLOPPY DISK.)

Hardware The parts of a computer that you can touch, such as the KEYBOARD, the MONITOR, and the DISK DRIVE, as well as all the parts inside.

High-level language High-level Computer languages are used for creating SOFTWARE and other PROGRAMS.

Industrial Revolution A very fast change in the way people lived during the late 18th Century in England when machines started being used to help people do their work.
Input DATA going into a computer.

Integrated circuit A 1958 invention that put all the circuits a computer needs in one place. The integrated circuit is the basis of the computer CHIP.

Jacquard, Joseph-Marie A French weaver and inventor who lived from 1752 to 1834.

Jacquard loom An automatic loom invented in 1801 by Joseph-Marie JACQUARD. It used instructions from punched cards to weave cloth.

Joystick An INPUT device. The joystick is attached to the computer. When you move the lever in any direction it sends a signal to the computer. A joystick may be used to make the moves in a game or to draw pictures on the screen. It is often used for games. Joysticks can be shaped like an airplane's control stick, a pistol grip without a pistol, or a handle on a pivot.

Keyboard The part of the computer that has keys like a typewriter. You use a keyboard to type INPUT into the computer. Each time you press a different key, a different signal is sent to the computer. A computer keyboard has some special keys that a standard typewriter doesn't have.

Laser printer A page printer in which a laser beam traces the image to be printed.

Leibnitz, Gottfried A German mathematician and inventor who lived from 1646 to 1716. He invented a hand-held mechanical CALCULATOR.

Mark I A very big computer built at Harvard University in 1943.

Memory The chips in a computer that store DATA and PROGRAMS. A computer has two different kinds of memory, RAM or ROM.

Monitor A TV-like device for displaying OUTPUT.

Output Information coming out of a computer.

Pascal, Blaise A French scientist, mathematician, and inventor who lived from 1623 to 1662.

Personal computer A computer made to be used by just one person, abbreviated as PC.

Portable Easy to carry around. Many PERSONAL COMPUTERS are portable. The size and weight of computers is getting smaller and smaller while their power is increasing.

Printer A machine that prints a computer's OUTPUT on paper. Two types are DOT-MATRIX and LASER PRINTERS.

Processing The actual work, or computing, done by a computer.

Program A set of instructions, written in COMPUTER LANGUAGE, that tells the computer what to do and how to do it. Programmers are the people who write these instructions, and programming is the name for what they do.

GLOSSARY

RAM Abbreviation for Random Access Memory: the part of the MEMORY that is erased when you shut the computer off. It holds the PROGRAM the computer is using.

ROM Abbreviation for Read Only Memory, the part of the MEMORY that is not erased when you turn the computer off. It gets the computer ready to use PROGRAMS.

Run To start using a PROGRAM.

Satellite A man-made machine that orbits the earth, moon, or another heavenly body. Satellites are often used to gather information.

Save To store DATA in a FLOPPY DISK or in MEMORY. You save information so that it will not be lost when you turn off the computer.

Scanner A machine that converts drawings, words, or other images into images that the computer can use.

Software The PROGRAMS used by a computer. Software is what runs on the HARDWARE.

Simulator Using a computer to practice or show activities that are similar to real activities.

Transistor A electrical device invented in 1948. It replaced the VACUUM TUBE, making computers smaller.

Vacuum tube A part of early ELECTRONIC devices like radios, TVs, and computers. Its wires were mounted in a glass tube with no air inside.

We'd like to hear from you!

Amica International is dedicated to producing the best in children's computer instruction books. We would like your comments regarding this book in order to help us plan and implement quality books in the future. Your comments are greatly appreciated.
Please take a moment to fill out this questionnaire and fax it to (206) 467-1522 or post it to:

Amica International
Attn: Children's Computer Book Division
1201 First Avenue South, Suite 203
Seattle, WA 98134

1. What age level do you think this book appeals to?
❍ 5-6 years ❍ 7-8 years ❍ 9-10 years ❍ 11-12 years ❍ 12 years +

2. How would you rate the readability of the book based on the age level you chose?
❍ very good ❍ good ❍ fair ❍ poor

3. Would you purchase another book similar to this one?
❍ yes ❍ no

4. How would you rate the quality of the illustrations?
❍ very good ❍ good ❍ fair ❍ poor

5. How would you rate the quality of the story?
❍ very good ❍ good ❍ fair ❍ poor

6. Do you like the size of the book (8 1/2 inches by 11 inches)?
❍ yes ❍ no
If your answer is no, what size would you recommend?

7. For this type of book, would you prefer:
❍ a hardback book ❍ a softcover book

8. Do you like the length of the book?
❍ yes ❍ no
If your answer is no, how many pages would you recommend?

9. Would you be more likely to purchase a book similar to this one if there was a computer disk included with the purchase price?
❍ yes ❍ no

10. Please indicate below other subjects you would like to see in a book similar to this one:
❍ DOS ❍ Windows ❍ PCs ❍ Macintosh
❍ Internet ❍ Paintbrush ❍ Spreadsheet ❍ Other: